J

INDIVIDUALIZED READING

INDIVIDUALIZED READING

A PRACTICAL APPROACH

SECOND EDITION

Richard C. Wilson, Ph.D.
Professor

Helen J. James, Ed.D.
Assistant Professor

**The University of West Florida
Pensacola**

KENDALL/HUNT PUBLISHING COMPANY
DUBUQUE, IOWA

Printed in the United States of America

Contents

Preface. vii

Acknowledgments ix

Chapter

   1.   Characteristics of Individualized Reading. 1

   2.   Providing Ample Books for Reading. 8

   3.   Book Reporting 16

   4.   Keeping Records 19

   5.   Grouping and Sub-Grouping 30

   6.   Assuring Skill Growth 36

   7.   Making the Change to Individualized Reading 41

   8.   Utilizing a Learning-Center Setting 45

   9.   Stepping Toward Individualizing 53

Bibliography. 59

Preface

Individualized reading has come to mean more than a way of teaching. It has been labeled a way of thinking about reading. It has become a means of encouraging and enabling pupils to read for their own purposes in a way that they develop a need to read and a confidence in their own abilities.

The authors of this book are not deluded into thinking that all teachers should be individualized reading teachers. They do believe in the strengths of the approach and the psychological bases underlying it.

It is the purpose of this book (a) to describe the essential features of an individualized reading program and (b) to explain the processes involved. It is hoped that the information will enable many teachers to recognize how this approach may replace their traditional reading programs without reducing attention to reading-skills instruction. It is further hoped that the explanations will encourage other teachers to supplement their present reading programs with a modified individualized reading program.

The first edition of this book appeared in 1965. Changes and additions have been made to incorporate the suggestions of teachers who have experienced a successful individualized reading program. The scope of the book has been extended to include recommendations for improved record-keeping and extensions of individualized reading both within and outside of the classroom.

R.C.W.
H.J.J.

To **Teachers,** in acknowledgment of their persistent search for better ways to meet the needs and interests of children.

Chapter 1

Characteristics of Individualized Reading

Individualized reading is an instructional approach which enables a teacher to guide children in developing initiative and personal responsibility for their own reading growth and refinement. As an approach, it may differ from traditional reading programs in several respects; yet, it includes the characteristics of good reading instruction. The major break with traditional procedures is the absence of a teacher's efforts to compel and coerce reactions of children to the contents of a single textbook.

This chapter provides an overview of the essential features of an individualized reading program, concluding with a statement of the major tenets of individualized reading. Succeeding chapters explain in detail the various components of the approach.

Free Access to Books and Materials

Teachers of individualized reading permit children free access to books of the children's own choice to be used in conjuction with a skills development program. The books are not limited to graded readers or books issued to "assure" a predetermined sequential development of skills applicable to the class or even a small portion of the class. There must be a choice and this is made possible by supplying a variety of books in terms of content and readability. Occasionally, children may select books that are too difficult or too easy for them. In those circumstances, the teacher may offer a choice of several books or stories he believes to be appropriate and still permit the child to make a selection from a realistic offering. Interest, ease of reading, and comprehension are the crucial factors in determining book selection for individualized readers.

Pupil Responsibilities

From the time a reading period may begin, children are permitted to leave their seats and tables for certain purposes. Sometimes they

1

exchange one book for another. At other times they record on a specially prepared form the completion of a selection. To simplify recording, some primary teachers have found it particularly convenient to place a poster board chart at some central place with library pocket charts attached. Each pocket has the name of a child on it. After completion of a given selection the child notes the title, author, and a simple comment, places this information on a card or slip of paper, and inserts it in the library pocket that has his name attached. Another practical way of recording a student's reading is to use a form similar to the one titled "Pupil's Record of Personal Reading" (Figure 1). The teacher may make copies of the form available by placing them in a small box, on the cover of which is a copy of the form so that children know without asking what is in the box. (Cigar boxes are ideal for this.) Children may complete and file this record at any convenient time without interfering with classroom routine.

Because pupils are occupied selecting books, reading, conferring with the teacher, reporting orally at given times, or recording notes about readings, there is less time for idleness upon completion of any particular task. Teachers may expect pupils who have been properly

---

Pupil's Record of Personal Reading

Name_____ Date _____

Title _____

Author_____ Book _____

Total Pages Read_____ Story _____

Other _____

Comment:

Figure 1.

guided to assume self-direction. As pupils gain confidence, they will routinely go about their tasks without reminders from the teacher.

In situations where some children are too immature to record their reading notes, another pupil or the teacher may help until such time as the necessary recording skills have been acquired. For mature pupils, especially those above grade three, teachers often provide a 3" x 5" file box for each pupil, appropriately labeled with name and contents; pupils may then record their reading notes and file their cards without assistance.

Immature pupils usually have more problems with self-directed work. It may be wise to use a "buddy system" until each pupil has learned and practiced all steps required to carry on the program. While making adjustments to the less teacher-dominated situation, a pupil may be guided by a friend, teacher's aide, or assigned "buddy" in selecting books, writing reactions to them, and keeping simple records.

It is the responsibility of the teacher to direct pupils into an acceptance of individual initiative. Training must be *planned* to lead children to understand how to use their time wisely without the constant and direct supervision of the teacher. In the initial stages of individualizing, there is need for reinforcement of good behavior and gentle redirection and reexplanation to change inadequate behavior. Time spent to establish good procedures will reduce the need for teacher interference at a later date, as pupils will aid each other because understandings have been developed.

The Individual Conference

When the individualized reading teacher confers with children about their reading, he appears pleasant, friendly, and especially interested in order to gain the necessary rapport for establishing mutual respect and trust. It is the purpose of the conference, of course, to get reactions from pupils that permit the teacher to make a proper evaluation of the skills listed on a sheet similar to the one entitled "Teacher's Record of Individualized Reading" (Figure 2), which appears on the following page. Simple opening statements that show a friendly curiosity about a given book or selection in a book often initiate responses that are usually sufficient to gauge children's understanding of what was read.

After rapport has been established, the teacher may probe for specific information and inferences resulting from reading. At intervals during the year, it is advisable to have pupils reread orally a portion of a selection. This is a proper time to note enunciation,

Teacher's Record of Individualized Reading Conferences

Name of Pupil

Book—Author (Note type of book)	Number of Last Page Read	Words Missed	Words* Missed Per 100	Silent Reading Compre-hension	Oral Reading	Rate	Word Recognition Skills Needing Attention	Date

*Five errors or more indicate the material is too difficult for free reading.

Figure 2.

phrasing, rate, intonation, regressions, decoding skills, and confidence. If, during a conference, a child appears to be upset, tense, or unresponsive, the teacher should postpone the conference until a time when conditions appear to offer greater opportunity for the child's achieving success.

The teacher may record with a simple code on Figure 2 to indicate a pupil's behavior. The words incorrectly read or omitted should be noted under "Words Missed." The teacher may use a plus (+) under the appropriate heading to denote superior comprehension and oral reading abilities. A check (✓) may mean average, expected, or normal responses. A minus (—) might represent gross misinterpretations, inability to discuss material read, or failure to understand the concepts or to read orally in a manner that would reveal comprehension. The symbols provide the teacher with a rather simple record of a pupil's responses during a conference.

Conditions for Progress

Since one of the important goals of all reading instruction, and especially individualized reading, is the development of an honest enjoyment of reading which leads to wide and varied reading, it is important to make the reading period one of the most enjoyable times of the school day. This is no time for chastising, admonishing, and shaming because a pupil is "not reading at the proper place," "reading too slowly," or "carelessly reading too fast." The greater the pleasure associated with reading, the more apt a youngster is to read; and that in itself leads to improved reading.

Unique Features

It is true that individualized reading programs vary a great deal in actual practice. The variations reflect differences in administrative policy and the relative emphasis upon skill growth, as well as personal characteristics of teachers.

Because of differences in the application of principles of individualized reading and the interpretations of terms in professional education, confusion sometimes occurs about the meaning of "individual differences." A competent teacher attempts to provide for the individual needs and interests of pupils, regardless of the reading approach employed. On a day-to-day basis, the teacher observes strengths and weaknesses of individual children and then builds into the ongoing program those activities which will promote growth. In the individualized reading approach, the teacher has extensive opportunities to note progress of individuals and to plan small-group activities to provide for special needs. Needs-meeting and goal-setting in terms of the learning rates and styles of individuals may be accomplished with ease if training in processes occurs in a suitable manner.

It is imperative that the teacher involve pupils in handling routine steps in the program. Control, order, and responsibility can be learned by most children if they are carefully guided. To be independent, children must have many opportunities to exercise independence. At the same time, they must have guidance at the crucial points in their growth toward independence.

The individualized reading approach makes possible and desirable children's assuming leadership functions and learning the satisfaction that comes from contributing to the success of a learning situation. Some of the leadership tasks are these: chairman of a small-group activity (needs or interests), classroom librarian, caretaker of a library table, part-time tutor, teacher's aide, director of a small research project, and file clerk. It makes sense to fit the task to the abilities of pupils, and it also makes sense to change tasks occasionally. The involvement of each pupil creates a feeling of personal worth that is important to the total enterprise.

Tenets

The individualized reading approach may be expected to include the following major tenets, which are apparent in current successful programs:

1. Every child is encouraged to select his own reading material for free reading and for skill growth.
2. The child may read at a pace he sets and not a pace established by a group leader.
3. There is no minimum or maximum amount of reading required for individuals or for a group.
4. There is no labeling of children in terms of reading ability. There are no high groups or low groups, no bluebirds or redbirds; and John and Susie have no groups named for them.
5. A child's ability to read is judged by the teacher in an individual conference or in a group organized for a specific reason. Evaluation is based upon performance with materials selected by pupils more often than with materials selected by the teacher.
6. Record keeping is a responsibility of the pupil as well as the teacher.

7. Skills are taught to individuals or to small groups as well as the total group when they are needed.

8. Oral reading is used for diagnosing reading needs of individual pupils. The data may be collected as children work in a group and confirm findings by reading specific sentences, as they read to each other or the total group a material selected expressly for oral reading, as they read during a conference to prove a point or to satisfy a request of the teacher, or as they read portions of selections to develop the interests of other children in a specific selection.

9. Silent reading is emphasized, the goals being to improve comprehension and rate and to encourage extensive individual reading.

10. Records kept by pupils and the teacher enable the teacher to know pupils' strengths and weaknesses and to plan appropriate activities in terms of needs and interests.

11. Curiosity about available reading materials is increased rather than diminished, since there are few occasions when pupils hear oral reading and discussion of selections which they will eventually read themselves.

12. Current commercially available materials and aids may be incorporated into the program for skills-learning, insuring a variety of activities and greater provision for children's needs and interests.

Chapter 2

Providing Ample
Books for Reading

Love for reading is not an inherited trait. It is not transmitted through the genes. It is a learned condition that thrives where reading is fostered by the example of others. A passion for reading is nurtured by the rewards that come as a child discovers that he can get meaning from print and can learn from printed materials. A habit need is created by an environment which insures many opportunities for reading and which contains reading materials in sufficient quantity and of sufficient variety to suit the needs, interests, and abilities of individual children.

Getting together a wide variety of books representing many levels of difficulty is a common problem with individualized reading. This is a problem primarily because children read more and often exhaust the usual sources of available books in a surprisingly short time. What a contrast this is to the regulation of reading by control of readers and other books to permit the stretching of materials so they may last throughout the school year.

The exhaustion of reading material, as paradoxical as it may seem, is one symptom of success with individualized reading. Of course, such a situation should not be allowed to persist, and it is the teacher's obligation to provide a remedy. There are a number of usually reliable sources of books. Some of them are rather self-evident; others are not so obvious.

The Library

It is probably quite natural to use the school library as a primary source of books. The supply may be ample but unavailable to teachers in quantity due to artificial restrictions placed upon library use. There are situations which tolerate only one visit to the library each week for individuals or classes. There are cases where a teacher may not withdraw sets of books from the library and then reissue them to his pupils for classroom use. Fortunately, most librarians, by the very nature of their dispositions and training, enjoy having pupils read avidly. Nothing seems to make them happier than to have many worn and tattered books upon shelves reflecting deterioration from constant use. Whenever librarians and teachers work together to permit a rapid turnover of available books for use in the individualized program, the supply is often adequate. Whether the teacher prefers to check books out himself or have pupils check them out individually from the library is a matter of individual taste and circumstance. The more mature pupils would probably gain by performing this rather perfunctory chore themselves. Physical conditions may also dictate one pattern or another. An extremely small library, constantly in use, might be a detriment to the non-scheduled use of its facilities.

Even in places where there is a good, well-stocked, open school library, a small classroom library is valuable to the individualized reading teacher. This is especially important to the primary teacher whose children may not have learned some of the locational skills essential to library work. Having books in children's classrooms offers the prospect of greater exposure, which induces curiosity and leads to browsing in free moments. Browsing, of course, is the forerunner to selection.

Less dependence is usually placed on non-school libraries. The public library is often too distant or inconveniently located for a large percentage of pupils, especially for very young children. When public libraries can be used, it is, of course, worthwhile to utilize them. If the public librarian is not at first inclined to lend books in quantity to a teacher for classroom use, it may be necessary to explain very carefully the purposes of borrowing and to inform the librarian the pupil population involved. Initial borrowing may be a small quantity for a short period of time. By sharing with the public librarian the results of adding materials to the classroom library, the teacher may gradually establish clear concepts of the value of lending books to trustworthy classroom teachers.

Basal Readers

Basal or graded readers and supplementary readers contain many interesting stories that have appeal to children when read under natural conditions. They are very useful for individualized reading. A supply of basal and supplementary readers, readily available without restriction, affords a ready-made source of wide variety. In recording readings in this type of book, some teachers have each story listed separately; this is especially suggested for beginning readers whose total reading vocabulary approximates that of the first to second reader level. Under these conditions a child may read a story in one reader and follow with a story in another. The readers the child selects may or may not be of the same readability. It would seem improper, however, to offer any adopted basal reader for free reading if there is a possibility the child may use that book later with another teacher in an ability-grouped program.

Trade Books from Home

Well-stocked book racks in variety stores, supermarkets, drugstores, newsstands, and other public places reflect the public's intense interest in reading. Many of these books are paperbacks. Thousands find their way into homes across the country daily. After one or two readings these books are often put aside and never touched again. Trade books of this sort may be donated or lent to the classroom for the mere asking. As usual, teachers must be selective and discard publications that for one reason or another make them unacceptable. A simple list of books lent to the class serves as a reminder that they should be returned to the owner at the end of the school session. It is probably advisable to accept all books without liability, and parents lending books should understand this clearly and preferably in writing. A source of books such as that described here can easily provide as many as several hundred good quality books for class use.

The Teacher Collection

The general public will never know, and perhaps appreciate less, the degree to which teachers contribute books and other reading materials for pupils that are teacher-financed. Nevertheless, most teachers have developed a rather respectable classroom library of their own. With a supplement by the teacher, few classrooms should postpone individualizing reading for lack of books.

Texts

Subject texts, such as those for the social studies, science, language arts, mathematics, and personal development, are normally used in terms of plans developed by the teacher. Functional reading skills are fostered through the location of specific data, the solution of problems, the analysis of information, and summarization. Even though reading skills are actually acquired from every type of reading, to use subject texts as a part of the individualized reading program could easily cause useless and unnecessary duplication. It is beneficial, however, to use texts as a part of individualized reading programs whenever such text material is not included in the teacher's requirements for the various curricula areas.

Book Orders

The lucky teacher sometimes has the pleasure of either helping the librarian make book orders or making a personal order financed by library funds. For this reason, sources of high interest, low vocabulary books are needed as well as sources needed by anyone looking for good books to stock a school or classroom library. Because books of all varieties have been coming out at a fantastic rate, booklists are barely released before they are practically obsolete. Nevertheless, it is helpful to have sources of good books within easy reach.

The American Library Association, The Association for Childhood Education International, and the H.W. Wilson Company provide booklists and recommendations for stocking and maintaining school and classroom libraries. *A Teacher's Guide to Children's Books* by Nancy Larrick might prove invaluable. Larrick's publication is offered by Charles E. Merrill Books, Inc., of Columbus, Ohio. Harcourt, Brace & Jovanovich, Inc., provide a convenient list of graded books entitled *A Graded List of Books for School Librarians.* This particular list categorizes selections into topics, grade level, usage for slow readers, and type sizes for sight-saving purposes.

It is extremely important to have books available at several levels of readability. A teacher should expect a range in most classrooms from two to four grade levels below and above the grade level of the individual classroom. For kindergarten and grade one, the teacher requires an abundance of picture books, many books at grade one level, and books above that level in sufficient quantity to meet the needs of all children.

A rule-of-thumb approach to estimating the range for a specific grade level is to figure two-thirds of the grade level, deduct that number from the grade level to find the bottom level, and add that number to the grade level to find the top level. For grade three, that would indicate the need of materials two grade levels below and two grade levels above grade three (i.e., two-thirds of three is two, and the range is one to five). For grade six, there would be need of materials between grade two level and grade ten level.

Since many teachers in grades seven through twelve have classes to which pupils are assigned according to abilities revealed by test scores, it is possible that they would have to experiment to identify the appropriate range of reading materials. Such teachers may be wise to place the interests of pupils ahead of readability in initial selections; then, when pupils' interests intensify, books of appropriate readability level may be added.

Many teachers and librarians, as well as clinicians, have found Spache's *Good Reading for Poor Readers* a valuable source of books that have high interest levels but low readability. The book is published by Garrard Publishing Company of Champaign, Illinois. Not only does this book offer information about trade books, but it also includes sections listing magazines and newspapers, textbooks, workbooks, and games. In addition, there are notes that should be helpful to the individualized reading teacher.

The Weekly Reader's Book Club and Scholastic's Arrow program enable teachers to make inexpensive paperbacks available to children. Regular announcements of available paperbacks are provided to teachers so that children may order and pay for personal copies throughout the school year. The bonus books included with paid orders help teachers build good classroom libraries.

With the increasing emphasis upon free reading or individualized reading as a central feature of the developmental reading plan, many publishers have responded by providing books ideally suited for taking care of the extremes in competencies usually met in most classrooms. Holt, Rinehart & Winston, Inc., has its Little Owl Series, which is unusually well adapted for individualized reading in the first and second grades. The Little Owl Series books vary in readability but are not labeled to permit a child to think of any of them as first grade, second grade, or any particular level of difficulty. The child determines for himself if any in the series is suitable for him. Harper, Row's "Torch" Series is also suitable for individualized reading programs in grades one, two and three.

Scott, Foresman and Company has developed what they call "Invitations to Personal Reading." This is a collection of 25 different titles per set providing a range of readability needed for children in most classes. Their plans call for providing sets of 25 books for various grade levels. The first set to appear is designed for the third grade. The books in the third grade set are categorized as: G—books that can be read by any child reading at third grade level, E—easy books, and A—advanced books.

The Carousel Book Program offered by the L.W. Singer Company is designed specifically for individualized reading programs. These selections have special appeal because of their emphasis upon esthetic, ethnic, and social values. The books are not coded for readability, but in general the Carousel Program is most suitable for the primary grades or for retarded readers in the fourth and fifth grades.

Few publishers have done more in the past several years to arouse preschoolers and beginning readers to the joy and curiosities of books than Random House/Singer, Inc. The Dr. Suess series is legend in many households and schoolrooms throughout the country. One who has watched a slow-learning fifth grader chuckling over *Green Eggs and Ham* realizes immediately the strong appeal this series has for children of almost any level of reading proficiency and grade level. With a vocabulary load comparable to certain pre-primers, Dr. Suess books invite and maintain reading interests without the structured and often sterile repetition often encountered in conventional basal stories written for beginning readers. Because of the popularity of this series and others like them, individualized reading often has its start in the home rather than in the school.

No publisher has presented a more carefully organized individualized reading "package" than Stone Educational Publications, Chicago. Their "Learning to Read while Reading to Learn" assortment may become a landmark for pre-packaged individualized reading programs.

Webster Division of McGraw-Hill Book Company publishes a "Classroom Science Series" which is inexpensive and easily adaptable to individualized programs. Garrard Publishing Company also publishes books of interest to young children that are inexpensive and useful for individualized programs.

Readability

Even though publishers frequently provide readability levels for special sets of books, most books in school libraries and classrooms are not labeled in terms of readability. To be certain children have free access to books of many levels of difficulty, an easy-to-use method for determining difficulty should be available to teachers using an individualized approach. Of course, no teacher is apt to spend an inordinate amount of time applying readability formulas to stacks of books to determine readability when simple observation can often tell her if her books are suitable for the children in her class. However, there are many instances when a teacher may wish to select a specific book for a given child because of its content and he then needs to know if the book is appropriate for that child in terms of difficulty.

For determining readability of materials used in primary grades, the University of Miami Readability Formula by Wheeler and Smith is especially useful because it is easy to apply. Directions for using are given in the November, 1954, issue of *Elementary English.*

Another formula for finding readability levels of primary materials is the Spache formula. Spache's formula is described in the March, 1953, issue of *The Elementary School Journal.*

The Dolch plan is also simple to use, and a teacher can use it to determine levels of readability from grades one through six. Directions and worksheets may be obtained from the Garrard Publishing Company, Champaign, Illinois.

Reading Levels

Reading specialists recognize four general levels of reading. They are the free or independent level, the instructional level, the frustration level, and the expectancy level. The individualized reading teacher is more concerned with the appropriateness of a book for the child's purposes in reading than the actual readability of a book as indicated by a publisher or a readability formula.

The best single guide to determine the suitability of a book for a child is the word-error count. Word errors are recorded by having a child read orally a passage of 100 to 200 words in length from his book. A 5% or greater error load (five words per 100, ten words per 200) indicates the material is too difficult even when help is available. Less than a 5% error load indicates the material is satisfactory for instructional purposes. The instructional level requires help from the teacher or a capable student-helper. An error load of 2% or less denotes the free level, a level the child may handle alone with little if any help. For older children, it has been found that, in practice, they may read with comprehension even when they exceed these suggested error loads; usually this occurs when they have already learned the basic concepts in the materials they are reading.

Few children will stick with a book very long when the error load exceeds 10%. Occasionally, a pupil's intense interest in a topic or subject will propel him to plug along at the frustration level. External motivation to locate important or needed information also has the effect of urging students to read material they might otherwise avoid.

Expectancy or capacity levels may be estimated by finding the grade level equivalent of the mental age determined from a reputable individually administered intelligence test. With the mental age known, subtract 5.5 (the common minimum entrance age for first graders) to approximate present expectency level. For example: if a child's M.A. is found to be 10 years, 6 months, subtract 5 years, five months, i.e., 10.6 less 5.5 = 5.1. This tells the teacher the pupil in question might read as well as the typical fifth grader in his first month of the fifth year in school. Because no mental measurement is without some culturally discriminating factors and the usual standard deviation, the M.A. grade equivalent should be supplemented by a listening comprehension test. For service purposes, the teacher may assume that a child's present expectancy level is equal to the highest level at which he comprehends about two thirds of the material when it is read aloud for him.

In determining error loads, count the following kinds of mistakes as errors:

1. A repetition of more than one word
2. The substitution of one word for another
3. The insertion of words not in the context
4. Reversal of the order of words or letters
5. Mispronunciations and requests for help (do not count regional variations or dialectic diverseness as errors)
6. The omission of letters, parts of words, or groups of words
7. Hesitations lasting from three to five seconds longer than the child's natural pauses between words or sentences
8. Gross neglect of punctuation signals

Chapter 3

Book
Reporting

A simple survey of friends and acquaintances is enough to reveal the widespread unpopularity of book reports. There is frequently an aura of distrust and suspicion when teachers require book reports as proof of reading; in addition, forcing children to read what the teacher dictates and then demanding a ritualized feedback appears to etch a distaste for good literature in the minds of many children and adults.

The traditional book report, which requires every child to illustrate his book or summarize his reading in a prescribed way, is not the way of individualized reading. Neither is the setting of an arbitrary quota of books to be read.

There are numerous ways to encourage children to share their reading with others. Creative teachers make available many alternatives, including both oral and written reports. With the many media now available, children can be creative in terms of their own needs and interests. Of course, one alternative should be the choice of simply recording the title of the book, the pages read, and the date the reading was completed. At times, children do not want to share what they read; also, they find some books lacking in qualities which make reporting valuable to themselves or others.

At some point in the child's educational program, he should be shown how to present a written book report. With teacher assistance, he can fill in a simple form that asks for a one-sentence summary or a short paragraph. He may also add his evaluation. Later, he may be asked to complete a more detailed report. It is essential, however, that the individualized reading teacher keep separate and discrete from sharing of children's self-selected reading the training needed for analyzing short stories and novels. There is no place in the individualized reading approach for detailed written reports describing characters, listing sequences of a plot, explaining a theme, or evaluating the author's style.

Reporting to the Class

If for every book a child read he were required to give an oral report before his classmates, disastrous results might be expected. The waste in time is apparent. The duplication of reports alone could easily consume an inordinate amount of the school day. A requirement of this sort tends to dampen a child's fervor for reading, and it might also become exceedingly tiresome to the class. One can easily imagine how disinterested children become with such a monotonous, routine exercise. They may well reason, "If I am to be punished for reading, I won't read."

Yet, boys and girls need the experience of sharing an enjoyable book with classmates. Some time in the daily or weekly schedule should be provided for children to talk to others about books. If several children have read the same book, have these children discuss the book. If some children are interested in a special topic or book about that topic, have them meet with a child or two who have read the particular book. These meetings can easily be arranged to coincide with the teacher's work in individual conferences and as adjuncts to the independent reading period.

Oral reports may be suggested by the teacher. He usually knows the children who have been deeply engrossed in reading certain books, and he also knows when to make appropriate remarks that are designed to incite children's desire to share with the group. There should be times when children volunteer to tell about personal reading without apparent motivation from any external source. This should be encouraged. For best results it is both wise and courteous to honor the child's willingness to report or not to report.

Older children enjoy taping their summaries or impressions of certain books. The organization of these productions is a valuable experience, for many study skills must be incorporated into one task. To enhance the presentations, children may supply either original drawings or pantomimes. In some instances, they create radio or television "talk shows" combining the reports on several books.

Enlivening Book Reporting

To encourage children's active, creative involvement in book sharing and reporting, the teacher should plan activities which reveal to children the many ways available to them for sharing. The teacher may demonstrate these to report his own reading, thereby promoting interest in certain books as well as enriching children's understandings of literature. At the same time, the teacher reveals a positive attitude toward both reading and sharing.

As children indicate eagerness to share what they have read, the teacher should make very clear the possible ways available to them. Frequently, what a child reports during the teacher-pupil conference gives clues to the way the child would like to share.

Individualized reading teachers have utilized many procedures to make informal book reporting more interesting and exciting. They have found that a routine format dulls interests and that variety kindles hidden desires to create unique productions. The following list includes some of the activities which have been successful:

1. Tape a book report prior to sharing time. Using the tape recorder permits a child to listen to his own report and also to watch the audience reaction to the report.
2. Use pantomime to animate certain parts of a book or to reveal traits of specific characters in a story.
3. Use a flannel board or a chart to illustrate significant events in a story or to describe conditions and scenes.
4. Dramatize by role-playing selected characters. When several children have read the same story, they may produce a skit of their choice. Young children should be expected to present a very brief skit, although even they may want to create an extensive production.
5. Present a story as a news report.
6. Discuss a picture or illustration which appears in a book.
7. Read orally a short stimulating part (not more than 200 words).
8. Illustrate a story in some manner (bulletin board display, transparencies, pictorial essay, puppetry, or mural).
9. Have small-group panel discussions (question and answer, "guess who," evaluations, or "We were there").
10. Create a radio or television program, utilizing audio-visual media.
11. Create a crossword puzzle to give major clues to parts of a story.
12. Create games requiring matching of titles of books with pantomimed enacting of roles. Children may create the games as well as the roles.

The teacher should expect to offer specific assistance to children as they prepare their reports. While providing examples of types of reports, the teacher may suggest to a few children that the materials they are presently reading might be shared in the way demonstrated. Once the children appreciate the values of sharing in many ways, the teacher can play a smaller and subtler role in making suggestions.

Chapter 4

Keeping
Records

Good teachers of reading have always kept ample records of their pupils' progress with a minimum amount of bookkeeping. They have maintained checklists to record evidence of skills gained, to reveal gaps in skills growth, and to provide data for special grouping. Frequently, they have had individual pupil folders in which they filed sample exercises, test results, summaries of books read and notes from observations and conferences.

The individualized reading teacher needs to view the keeping of records as an integral part of instruction. The teacher's significant record keeping occurs during conferences with individual children or small groups; the pupil's record keeping occurs as he completes reading tasks. In both instances, data is recorded immediately, preventing the loss of information that results when there is a delay in writing evaluations. Thus, teachers and pupils alike come to view their records as related, essential aspects of individualized reading.

The purpose of record keeping becomes clear as teachers share records with pupils. When a child is guided to set appropriate short-term goals for himself after studying his current status as indicated by available records, he is more likely to appreciate the reasons for conferences, small-group activities, and record keeping itself. For many children, the teacher's explanations of their needs based on evidence they helped to provide brings about positive changes of attitudes and improved study habits. An ultimate goal should be the transfer of responsibility to the pupil for the selection of skills to be learned, an outcome made possible by demonstrating the relationship of skills to progress.

To make record keeping palatable, only simple, useful, essential types of records should be maintained. In this chapter are suggestions which should enable a teacher to record data and to plan adequately for all children in a classroom.

Quantitative Summary of Individual Reading

Student: _____

Year: _____

Month	Books 1-50 pp.	Books 51-100 pp.	Books Over 100 pp.	Stories and Articles	Total
September					
October					
November					
December					
January					
February					
March					
April					
May					
June					
Totals					
Summer					

Figure 3.

The Child's Record

Each child should complete a simple record whenever he reads a book, story, or article. A sample copy of the form, described in chapter one, may be attached to the lid of a container where children may deposit their reports. An adequate supply of the forms should be placed in a convenient location so that children may obtain them easily.

At given intervals, perhaps once or twice monthly, the children's reports should be collected and quickly tabulated on a summary sheet. A sample form entitled "Quantitative Summary of Individual Reading" (see Figure 3) appears in this chapter. The teacher then has information about the amount and type of reading each child has reported.

It is advisable to meet with the pupil occasionally to review the number and types of books the child has reported on his own initiative. Care should be taken to avoid undue emphasis on numbers alone. Many teachers have found that credit for "numbers of books" may lead to artificial competitiveness and a tendency to make false reports.

The Teacher's Record

At each individual teacher-pupil conference, the teacher should record specific information about the child's reading. Information is needed about vocabulary knowledge, reading rate, silent reading comprehension, oral reading proficiency, interests, and other factors encompassing word-attack skills, study skills, and selection of materials. A form of this type was described in chapter one. It should be clear that, in any single conference, only selected items of information should be collected.

Forms such as these are cumulative, providing clear evidence of changes in behavior over a period of time. They also may serve as the basis for decisions about grouping children for short-term skills instruction.

Record keeping is simple and efficient if the teacher keeps the individual conference report in a separate folder for each child. In addition, notes of observations made while children are working, samples of completed exercises, and other comments may be placed in the folder for later reference. The folder may be the standard filing folder or a teacher-made folder. Some teachers construct folders by joining two 9" x 12" pieces of construction paper with transparent or masking tape.

Record of Individual Pupil Conferences

Name of Pupil	Week Beginning	Week Beginning	Week Beginning	Week Beginning	Week Beginning
	M T W T F	M T W T F	M T W T F	M T W T F	M T W T F
	M T W T F	M T W T F	M T W T F	M T W T F	M T W T F
	M T W T F	M T W T F	M T W T F	M T W T F	M T W T F
	M T W T F	M T W T F	M T W T F	M T W T F	M T W T F
	M T W T F	M T W T F	M T W T F	M T W T F	M T W T F
	M T W T F	M T W T F	M T W T F	M T W T F	M T W T F
	M T W T F	M T W T F	M T W T F	M T W T F	M T W T F
	M T W T F	M T W T F	M T W T F	M T W T F	M T W T F
	M T W T F	M T W T F	M T W T F	M T W T F	M T W T F
	M T W T F	M T W T F	M T W T F	M T W T F	M T W T F
	M T W T F	M T W T F	M T W T F	M T W T F	M T W T F
	M T W T F	M T W T F	M T W T F	M T W T F	M T W T F
	M T W T F	M T W T F	M T W T F	M T W T F	M T W T F
	M T W T F	M T W T F	M T W T F	M T W T F	M T W T F
	M T W T F	M T W T F	M T W T F	M T W T F	M T W T F
	M T W T F	M T W T F	M T W T F	M T W T F	M T W T F
	M T W T F	M T W T F	M T W T F	M T W T F	M T W T F
	M T W T F	M T W T F	M T W T F	M T W T F	M T W T F

Figure 4.

Frequency of Conferences

A record is also needed to indicate the dates of teacher-pupil conferences so that the teacher can control the frequency of conferences. Without this record, it is possible that some children will receive more consideration than they need and that others may be neglected. At a glance, a teacher should be able to determine the recency and frequency of individual meetings with children. A record of conferences like the one titled "Record of Individual Pupil Conferences" (see Figure 4) helps the individualized reading teacher determine how her time is spent, how it might be spent, and whom she has been helping. By circling the day of the week each conference is held, the teacher has an up-to-the-minute record of conferences at her fingertips.

This record of recency and frequency of conferences should be placed in the teacher's notebook for handy reference. The teacher may not only avoid overlooking children who need help but also have the evidence to show children who may demand more than their share of the teacher's time.

There are always children who seem to want much interaction with others about their reading. When a teacher discovers these children, he can arrange special-interests groups, pairing of children, or panel discussions. Most children will respect the teacher's decisions about scheduling of individual conferences if adequate plans are made to permit sharing.

Record of Skills Lessons

There is hardly a better way to grow in reading skills than to read a lot. Individualized reading is designed to encourage just that. Not many teachers, however, wish to depend on chance alone to assure skills growth in reading and especially in the category of word-attack skills. For this reason, it is necessary for most teachers to prepare a list of the reading skills that he believes suitable for his pupils and to develop a plan to include instruction in the daily or weekly schedule.

Teachers have found it difficult to classify skills in terms of appropriate levels, whether using a manual to a basal series or a professional text listing sequences of skills. Some have solved the problem by utilizing a curriculum guide or a catalog of reading objectives. Many have found that they could develop a list of needed skills and teach most of them during regularly scheduled skills periods, taking care to correlate them with language activities which make sense to the children.

It might be helpful to organize the word-attack skills in categories, as shown on the sample form labeled "Record of Skills Lessons in Word Attack" (see Figure 5). It might also be helpful to develop at least three different lesson plans for each skill the teacher believes important for his pupils. As the lessons are completed, the teacher need record only the date the specific lesson was presented.

A Reading Skills Check Sheet

Many teachers in an individualized reading program feel more comfortable with an outline of the essential ingredients of a balanced reading program. Figure 6 illustrates a simple chart which serves to remind the teacher of the many general factors to be considered in teaching at any level.

The blocks permit the teacher to record the source of a particular lesson about a given skill that his children need. For example, the block under Wednesday might have the following notation: "Health Teacher's Manual, *Meadow Gold*, p. 79—ideas for teaching s and h sounds."

It is not necessary or even desirable for the teacher to feel any compulsion to have entries in every block for every week. This weekly record form is just a reminder of the skills normally taught in a good reading program and serves as a handy reference for ideas and ready-made plans to aid the teacher. The last column is provided so that the teacher may enter the names of students who appear to need further help on specific skills taught or re-taught during the week.

As children gain independence in locating skills exercises to meet their needs, they may assist the teacher in listing good available sources. Over a period of time, the teacher may then develop a very comprehensive listing of suitable sources for a variety of skills.

Reading Skills Growth Record

A simple grid like the one in Figure 7, entitled "Reading Skills Growth Record," is very useful for registering specific skills or topics. These items may be a simple reference to titles, pages, chapters, or sections in a text; or they may be the teacher's own list of skills taken from a catalog of reading objectives.

Many similar grids may be used with various areas of reading and language arts. For spelling, the numbers may indicate chapters in the spelling text. In any event, the form permits the recording of skills growth and objective attainment at a pace comfortable and desirable for the pupil rather than the teacher.

As illustrated in Figure 7, a check ($\checkmark$) can be used to indicate satisfactory learning of the skill. A cross ($\times$) can show that further

Record of Skills Lessons in Word Attack

Structural Analysis			
Item	1st Lesson	2nd Lesson	3rd Lesson
Compound Words			
Contractions			
Inflections			
Roots and Stems			
Prefixes			
Suffixes			
Syllabication			
Phonetic Analysis			
Initial Consonants			
Final Consonants			
Rhyming			
Blends			
Consonant Digraphs			
Hard/Soft c and g			
Phonograms			

Figure 5.

Phonetic Analysis (Cont.)			
Item	1st Lesson	2nd Lesson	3rd Lesson
Short Vowels			
Long Vowels (silent -e)			
Complex Vowels			
Long Vowels (Digraphs)			
Diphthongs			
Schwa			
Generalizations			
Visual Clues to Accent			
Open, Accented Syllables			
Closed, Accented Syllables			
Two-Syllable Words Ending in -le			
Silent -e (One-Syllable Words)			
Vowel Digraphs			

Figure 5. (Con't.)

Reading Skills Check Sheet

Week Beginning _____ Weekly Record

Group or
Section _____

Item	Mon.	Tues.	Wed.	Thurs.	Fri.	Pupils Needing Extended Work
Context Clues						
Phonetic Analysis						
Structural Analysis						
Syllabication						
Accent						
Roots and Stems						
Dictionary Skills						
Silent Reading Comprehension						
Oral Reading						
Free Reading						
Critical Reading						
Content Reading (Subject Matter)						
Rate Building						
(Other)						

Figure 6.

Reading Skills Growth Record

Pupils' Names	Skills Areas															
	1	2	3	4	5	6	7	8	9	10	11	12	13	14	15	16
	Compound Words	Root Words	Prefixes	Suffixes	Syllables	(etc.)										
John Adams																
Fred Brown																
Ralph Cole																
Sue Doan																
Frances Gay																
Bill Gray																
Martha Hall																
Sam House																
Jerri Johnson																
Gail Jones																
Michael Kraft																
Ann Lane																
Tom Locke																
Bob Loren																
Sally Lutz																
(etc.)																

Figure 7

work is needed. When a satisfactory level of performance is reached on a skill previously shown as unsatisfactory (×), the cross then can be circled to show subsequent attainment. A record such as this makes it easy for a teacher to see at a glance those pupils who need additional study or help on a particular skill.

Interrelationships of Records

As teachers collect evidence of children's reading abilities, they begin to note patterns of various types. Some children appear to learn skills easily, even almost automatically, while others seem to have more difficulty. Many children read materials pertaining to one or two interests, whereas some may read almost anything; some read many books or stories, and some do not find reading exciting.

As the records begin to reveal information, the teacher may note that the child who does not seem to learn skills rapidly is also the child who does not read many stories. Or, he may observe that the child who seems to be low in vocabulary sticks to one subject most of the time. With such evidence, the teacher is in a position to commence diagnostic teaching in earnest. He knows strengths and weaknesses of particular children, and he can plan lessons which test his estimates of their needs. On a week-to-week basis, he can collect more data and revise his plans so that most children are making progress.

The essential ingredients of the individualized reading approach should not be forgotten, especially when the teacher acquires sufficient information for diagnostic teaching. Children must be free to select their own materials, to proceed at their own pace, and to make decisions about their program. Children must not feel coerced or threatened. It is believed that *careful* sharing of the child's records and the teacher's records can create confidence in both the approach and the teacher, with the result that children will seek materials which will help them overcome their weaknesses.

Chapter 5

Grouping and
Sub-Grouping

Grouping is a very popular topic among teachers. Controversies over grouping and the reasons for grouping appear to be endless. This may be true because administrators and teachers give many different reasons for grouping.

One cause of confusion may be that grouping is sometimes viewed as synonymous with teaching practices. Grouping is not a method; neither is grouping an end in itself. Rather, grouping is a means to an end, an organizational aid or procedure designed to permit teachers to make better provisions for the needs of pupils. Once a group has been formed, regardless of the basis or criteria, the activities that take place are of much greater importance than such details as the numbers in the group, the sex of group members, the grade placement of individuals, or the general abilities of group members. Actually, the nature of an activity should determine the type of group to be arranged.

Another cause of confusion may have been an assumption that individualizing as an approach eliminates grouping. There are a few schools that have established programs which enable children to work alone consistently; usually, such schools require extra personnel to diagnose pupils' needs and to prescribe lessons, units, or activities. That concept of individualization differs from the concept applicable to the individualized reading approach.

Grouping as a procedure should be understood as essential to a strong individualized reading program. To provide interaction among children, reinforcement of ideas, and refinement of concepts and skills, the teacher must form small, flexible, short-term groups whose members are aware of the specific purposes for grouping. Children may become members of several types of groups within a short span of time, each group designed to provide for a specific need or interest.

Group Permanence

The basis for grouping smaller numbers in a classroom for some special purpose stands in contrast to the reasons for grouping in many conventionally organized classrooms. There is no facade of permanence for groups using individualized reading. Because the life expectancy of a group may last no longer than a single meeting of less than 30 minutes duration, it becomes illogical to imply perpetuity by labeling with titles like John's group, the Bluebirds, Group II, the slow-reading group, or any other name.

Grouping makes sense only in terms of immediate purpose in an individualized approach. A teacher who says, "I would like the seven boys and girls who need extra help on recognizing base words to meet with me around the work table for a few minutes," is establishing a clear purpose for the formation of a sub-group. This teacher knows certain children need help on special things and the smaller groups are established to deal with those needs. When groups are formed for a definite purpose to facilitate instruction, they are justifiable. Otherwise, there are no defensible reasons for forming a special group.

Values of Grouping

There are values inherent in small-group work. Instructional plans should be based on these values, no matter what the nature of the over-all reading program happens to be:

1. Many children participate more actively within small groups than within a larger one. The "auditorium" effect is lessened.
2. Often, children need to share ideas with others who have an interest in the same books or other reading materials.
3. The small group facilitates greater interaction between the teacher and individual pupils.
4. The exchange and sharing of materials can be accomplished with greater ease in a small group.
5. Children receive reinforcement almost immediately, either from other children or from the teacher's acceptance or correction of responses.
6. Children learn responsibilities of leadership and cooperation in connection with designated tasks.
7. Both oral language and concept development can be encouraged because there is an opportunity for each child to contribute his ideas, to clarify ideas, and to hear ideas of others.

Same Interest, Same Book

Adults and children enjoy sharing reactions and comments about stories and books. It is not unusual to find people discussing for hours a particular book they have read. Because there is so much pleasure to be had by reacting to the same literature, this basis for forming a small group is one of the soundest. "Fred, Sam, Bob, Billy, Gail, and Dick are all interested in spaceships," says one teacher, "and I have six copies of a book on this subject. You folks may take them and some day very soon we should meet and discuss what we have read. Perhaps there are some things in here that might interest the rest of the class." When the time comes to meet with the six who read or are still reading about spaceships, the balance of the class are engaged in their own independent, self-selected free reading.

Some teachers have found the "buddy system" helpful to keep immature or restless students gainfully involved while focusing principally on another segment of the class. The "buddy system" or pairing, as it is sometimes called, encourages children to share on a one-to-one basis and to help each other. Often the partners work in a parallel manner by reading or researching independently but in physical proximity of each other.

Same Interest, Different Books

It is not always convenient for a teacher to have multiple copies of the same book. Interest groups, however, are easily formed by using different books though all may be about the same general topic. It is just as interesting to share information and comment from six sources about spaceships as from a single common source. This procedure affords the extra advantage of providing the materials to children according to reading ability if the materials themselves vary in their readability. A small group in which each child has a different book offers the extra reward of greater depth and breadth of subject content.

"I thought it would be interesting for us to meet for a while and discuss our books about spaceships and outerspace," a teacher might say, "and share a bit of information we have collected. Bill has learned a lot about solid fuel propellents, Frances has discussed gravitational effects on flight with me, and David has spoken to me about the Van Allen Belt. Who would like to begin our discussion by telling us something unusual or interesting about his findings?"

An approach such as the one described usually includes some oral reading of brief descriptive passages to clarify points or to reveal greater detail. The teacher may or may not remain with the group to

guide or direct it. She might well leave the assemblage under the
guidance of a chairman if she feels a greater need to move around the
room, help individuals, or work with another small group to get it
under way.

Skills Groups

The individualized reading teacher who has a well-developed plan
for teaching the skills of reading often finds it worthwhile to form
small temporary groups of students to work on a specific attainment.
Many teachers have long recognized the waste involved when teaching the entire class a principle or generalization in cases where many
pupils already have a mastery of that specific principle or generalization.

The most effective time to teach a skill comes when the child feels
a need for it. Obviously, teachers cannot be with every child each
time he meets a reading problem. Most teachers, physical limitations
notwithstanding, are not prone or able to interject into a normal day
periodic individual skills lessons that are satisfactorily comprehensive
in nature.

Skills groups should be based upon recognized pupil needs. Sub-
groups may be considered adjuncts to the total-class diagnostic skills
teaching program rather than a substitute for it.

A Listening Group

To enhance the skills of audience reading, refine oral reading skills
through practice, and gain esteem and recognition in the eyes of
peers, what is more appropriate than having a child read before a
small group? Reading of this variety may take a number of forms.

A child may be encouraged to read the most exciting part of a
selection to a group. The teacher should judiciously determine the
appropriateness and length of the reading by one child for a single
sitting. Others should have equal opportunity to read but without
the pressure of a requirement. Care should be taken to assure a
child's capability of reading with ease his selection for oral reading. If
a child plods along, he doesn't hold the interest and respect of his
audience very long.

There can be no limit set on the number of small groups formed
for listening to pupils read. Two or more groups may well function
simultaneously. On many occasions it may be wise to form a single
small group while the majority of the class are busily occupied with
their own reading.

Listening to others discuss or read short selected portions of books can be a stimulating experience if skillful questioning by the teacher increases interest and promotes critical reading. Teachers who occasionally tease, challenge pupils to prove their points, and encourage friendly controversy and a free exchange of opinion are frequently the most successful in developing worthwhile listening groups. As pupils come to question writers, sources, dates, qualifications, and authority in lieu of glibly accepting as "the final word" whatever they see in print, they improve in reasoning abilities and support their conclusions with clear statements or references to their sources.

Creative reading also finds an outlet in a listening group. When a child extends, modifies, re-interprets, colors, limits, or otherwise stretches the meaning and original exposition, he reveals growth in creative reading skills. Listening to one child's discussion enables other children to understand that each person creates a unique mental image from what he reads. Divergency of thinking is thus stimulated and supported.

Features of Individualized Grouping

All of the reasons for grouping may not be included in this discussion, but enough are given to point up its need and importance. Grouping is just as essential for individualized reading as for any other arrangement. The features of grouping in this type of reading program may be analogous to the reasons sometimes given for grouping in other types of reading programs. There are, however, a few unique traits applicable to small-group work in an individualized reading situation:

1. All groups are temporary.
2. Membership in a group is based upon common needs or interests.
3. Each group is called together for a specific purpose, made clear immediately.
4. Group meetings are scheduled according to needs, usually as an outgrowth of teacher-pupil interaction and frequently as a result of teacher-pupil planning.
5. Procedures followed by each group will vary according to the purpose of the group.
6. Many groups will select one of their members as chairman, thereby relieving the teacher of the leadership role.
7. Discussions about reading selections result from pupils' interests in a topic rather than their having read specific pages in a book.

It can be seen that there will be no long-range scheduling of group meetings based on a school calendar. Also, there will be no predetermined or set pattern of procedures, nor will there be stable groups for any purpose.

It should be remembered that good grouping practices, like good teaching, will foster differences and divergent thinking rather than uniformity and conformity. In the individualized reading approach, good grouping practices will also foster independence.

Chapter 6

Assuring
Skill Growth

Traditionally, word-attack and comprehension skills have been taught as they appeared in guidebooks or manuals that accompanied structured reading programs. For children whose instructional reading levels were compatible with the classroom text, this may have worked satisfactorily. For the many children whose instructional levels were incompatible with the classroom text, reading has been accompanied by frustration, negativism, and the rejection of reading as a pleasant and worthwhile activity.

Diagnostic Approaches

Skill growth with individualized reading is closely associated with a diagnostic procedure. Rather than routinely teaching a skill to prepare for future reading tasks, the individualized reading teacher checks to see which skills are needed.

Obviously, few teachers feel competent enough to rely solely on their personal judgments of which word-attack and comprehension skills should be or should not be taught and when they should be taught. The placement of skills at various levels in structured programs attests to the lack of agreement of the most appropriate place to introduce them. It is unreasonable to believe the placement of a specific word-attack or comprehension technique in an established order would fit the individual requirements of all children even if there were general agreement on the order in which skills should appear.

Rather than associate skills with specific grade levels, the individualized reading teacher often thinks of skills needed for immature, mature, and highly gifted readers in his class. By categorizing the skills found in manuals or a course of study, he may then provide instruction in appropriate reading skills for the pupils needing them.

For illustrative purposes only, there are presented the following examples of three groups of reading skills to be attained. Those appropriate for immature readers have been placed in Group I; for mature readers, in Group II; and for gifted readers, in Group III. This list should not serve as a basic guide for a teacher but only as a prototype or model for skills grouping. The pupils' ages, their backgrounds of experience, and their achievement during prior years should be considered when skills are selected for each type of reader.

Group I

1. Use of picture clues to infer meanings.
2. Use of word context clues to make reasonable guesses of word meanings.
3. Ability to decode single consonants in initial, medial, and final positions.
4. Ability to analyze unknown words by substituting consonants from known words.
5. Ability to decode consonant blends, such as *bl, br, st, sm, rt, ng.*
6. Use of phonograms or linguistic patterns, such as *ab, ac, et, in, op, um.*
7. Ability to recognize main ideas, sequence, and implications in a simple story.
8. Knowledge of spelling patterns which indicate long vowel sounds (silent -*e* principle, consonant-vowel as in *go,* vowel digraphs).
9. Knowledge of short vowel sounds.
10. Knowledge of spelling patterns which indicate short vowel sounds (vowel-consonant, consonant-vowel-consonant).
11. Knowledge of speech sounds of *wh, sh, ch,* and *th.*
12. Knowledge of silent letters, such as *k* or *g* before *n, w* before *r.*
13. Sight recognition of most of the high frequency words, such as those in the Dolch 220 Word List or the Kucera-Francis 220 Word List (the latter an updating of the Dolch list).
14. Knowledge of simple inflections, such as *s* or *es* for plural of nouns, *ed* for past tense of verbs.
15. Ability to decode compound words and contractions.

Group II

1. Knowledge that every syllable has a vowel sound.
2. Ability to form syllables by dividing words between double consonants which appear between vowels (rab-bit, can-non, rad-dish).
3. Knowledge that a single vowel in a closed accented syllable will usually have the short sound.

4. Ability to form syllables by dividing words before single consonants which appear between vowels (la-dy, pa-per, stu-pid).
5. Knowledge that there are exceptions to the fourth skill (e.g., hon-or, lim-it).
6. Ability to give the soft or hard sound for *c* and *g* on the basis of visual clues (*ce, ci, cy, ge, gi, gy* for soft sounds; *ca, co, cu, ga, go, gu* for hard sounds; exceptions of *get, give*).
7. Ability to state main ideas, sequence, and implications in a reading selection of three to seven pages.
8. Ability to decode long words by using meanings of prefixes and suffixes.
9. Knowledge of generalizations about certain vowel digraphs (ai, ee, ie, oa, ui).
10. Knowledge of generalizations about -*e* at the end of a one-syllable word (causes the vowel in the vowel-consonant-*e* pattern to have the long sound; causes the final consonant in the vowel-consonant-consonant-*e* pattern to have a soft sound, as in else, pulse, fringe).
11. Ability to decode common diphthongs, such as *oi, oy, ou, ow*.
12. Ability to use the pronunciation key in a dictionary to achieve correct pronunciation of unknown words.
13. Ability to arrange words in alphabetical order.
14. Understanding of special orthographical devices (punctuation, italics, special symbols such as diacritical marks).
15. Understanding of simple idioms, such as "sharp as a tack," "light as a feather."

Group III

1. Understanding of visual clues indicating an accented first syllable (two-syllable words which do not contain two vowels in the second syllable).
2. Understanding that an accent may shift in words to which prefixes or suffixes are added.
3. Ability to form syllables and give the correct vowel sound for two-syllable words that end in -*le* (the consonant before -*le* goes with the -*le*; if the resulting first syllable is open, the vowel is long; if the resulting first syllable is closed, the vowel is short).
4. Understanding that the dictionary provides common pronunciations, word origins, meanings, synonyms, antonyms, and parts of speech.
5. Understanding of heteronyms (same spelling but different accents such as CON-struct, con-STRUCT).

6. Use of meanings of roots as an aid to vocabulary growth.
7. Understanding of meanings of roots acquired from other languages.
8. Interpretation of figurative language and idioms.
9. Understanding of transition words, such as *next, but, or, on the other hand, in spite of that, in addition*).
10. Ability to restate the main idea and to provide supporting details.
11. Ability to summarize a selection, including giving correct sequence, and to infer subsequent actions or ideas.
12. Ability to adjust rate of reading to accommodate the purposes of reading and the nature of the material.
13. Ability to generalize as a result of reading a selection.
14. Ability to use the library card catalogue to locate sources on a specific topic.
15. Understanding that critical reading requires a questioning and evaluating attitude concerning the author's competency, the recency of information, ambiguity, propaganda, bias, and the appropriateness and logic of a selection in terms of its purposes.

Workbooks and Skill Growth

Workbooks offer the reading teacher an avenue to reap the advantages of structure without compromising a basic principle of individualized work. Many of the newer workbooks that are not adjuncts to basal programs lend themselves to use in an individualized skills development program.

When workbooks are used as a follow-up activity to a large-group presentation, the principles of individualized skill growth are maligned. When each child progresses in structured material at the pace he himself establishes and works with material that he needs, the principles of individualized work are affirmed.

The task of placing a child with structured material he needs is not a difficult one. The first step is simply locating the child's operating or instructional reading level. Step two is matching the instructional level with the corresponding level workbook; the child proceeds with help from his teacher or a classmate at appropriate times. This procedure requires a supply of workbooks, preferably the re-usable type, at several grade levels, in contrast to the practice of supplying the same level material for all members in a single classroom.

Balance in the Skills Program

To neutralize the tendency to teach those elements of language which have greater appeal to students and teachers at the expense of other essential learnings, some kind of balance should be established in the reading program. Charts such as those depicted in Figures 6 and 7 in chapter four are designed to help maintain a reasonable balance in the weekly program.

Of course, no one should assume the presentation of lessons on the ten or more skills listed for every day of the week or for every week in the school month. The spaces are provided for the teacher to make notations about teaching techniques (see Figure 6) or pupils' progress (see Figure 7). Typically, the entries in Figure 6 would reflect a scatter of selected sources or techniques rather than a grid filled with activities and work for each day and on each topic.

Chapter 7

Making the Change
to Individualized Reading

As soon as a child has developed a sight vocabulary of several hundred words, he is ready to move rapidly into an individualized reading program. Without sufficient sight vocabulary, he cannot read primer-level materials independently; with several hundred words that he can recognize, he can read many stories and books alone. The teacher must collect and offer many book choices that have enough appeal to sustain independent reading.

Individualized reading is a partner of the language-experience approach. Many teachers initiate their reading programs by recording common experiences during the first few weeks of school. This approach may be as effective with older children as with younger children. Even college graduate students benefit from rereading notes and transcriptions reflecting interpretations and records of earlier learning. At any level, the language-experience technique may serve as an adjunct and initiator of wide individualized reading.

For teachers operating along traditional lines, the timing and manner of transferring to this new program may cause concern. When to make a change and how much change to make are important considerations.

Which is best, combining basal-reader groups with individualized reading, making a deliberate and gradual change, or changing quickly and completely to the new program? These are three choices for the teacher who may be charting a transition from one way of organizing and conducting a reading program to individualized reading.

Combined Basal Series and
Individualized Reading

Because of reservations some teachers have about individualized work, they might prefer to maintain the basal-grouping plan in combination with individualized reading. For teachers using the three-

41

group organization for reading, a schedule similar to the following might prove beneficial.

Monday—Three reading groups as usual.

Tuesday—Groups for "slow" and "average" readers. Individualized reading for "advanced" readers.

Wednesday—Groups for slow readers. Individualized reading for average and advanced reading.

Thursday—Groups for average readers. Individualized reading for low and advanced readers.

Friday—Individualized reading for all children.

Using the plan described above as a starting point, it is relatively simple to increase or decrease the amount of time given to individualized reading. A balanced daily plan should consider the following:

1. Time to select and exchange books and to permit brief book "talks" when appropriate.
2. Twenty to sixty minutes for free reading (which may vary from day to day and is considerate of the maturity of the children).
3. Skills development time to work with individuals, small groups, or the total group as needed.
4. A conference period for working with individuals or small groups for the purpose of analyzing individual reading skills.

Utilizing cues from children, the teacher may decide to make a gradual change from this plan to a completely individualized program. The decision should be based on both the teacher's confidence and the pupils' abilities to learn the new procedures.

The Gradual Change

For a more gradual induction into individualized reading, providing a convenient schedule, the plan suggested by the chart on the following pages (Figure 8) might be more appropriate. It allows for as much as a six-week period to complete conversion from the basal-reader, ability-group plan to the individualized plan.

The Rapid Change

For a teacher employing the ability-group pattern, it may be wiser to make the switch with one group at a time. In this manner adjustments to a new routine are minimized.

Because high-ability children are likely to adapt more rapidly to change, the initial step may very well be made with them. At the time usually reserved for reading with the "fast" group, the teacher

A Suggested Plan for a Six-Week Transition to Individualized Reading

Monday	Tuesday	Wednesday	Thursday	Friday	Group	Week
G-R	G-R	G-R	I-R	I-R	High	First
G-R	G-R	G-R	G-R	G-R	Average	
G-R	G-R	G-R	G-R	G-R	Low	
G-R	G-R	I-R	I-R	I-R	High	Second
G-R	G-R	G-R	I-R	I-R	Average	
G-R	G-R	G-R	G-R	G-R	Low	
G-R	I-R	I-R	I-R	I-R	High	Third
G-R	G-R	I-R	I-R	I-R	Average	
G-R	G-R	G-R	I-R	I-R	Low	
I-R	I-R	I-R	I-R	I-R	High	Fourth
G-R	I-R	I-R	I-R	I-R	Average	
G-R	G-R	I-R	I-R	I-R	Low	
I-R	I-R	I-R	I-R	I-R	High	Fifth
I-R	I-R	I-R	I-R	I-R	Average	
G-R	I-R	I-R	I-R	I-R	Low	
I-R	I-R	I-R	I-R	I-R	High	Sixth
I-R	I-R	I-R	I-R	I-R	Average	
I-R	I-R	I-R	I-R	I-R	Low	

I-R = Individualized Reading
G-R = Guided Reading (Basal Readers)

Figure 8.

simply says something like this. "Today I want you to read from the books you have selected from the reading table. When I call you, come to me for a few minutes. I would like to know what your selection is about, how well you read it, and how much you enjoy it."

During the individual conference, which may last only five minutes or even less, the teacher records information about the child's reading on the teacher's record of individual conferences (see Figure 2 in chapter 1). The pupil is then asked to record the needed information about title, author, and pages read on a card (see Figure 1 in chapter 1) when he finishes reading the book.

At the end of several days, the teacher can tell at a glance the number and types of books each child has been selecting. Also, from the comments noted in the teacher's record, it is possible to evaluate each child's progress. The record serves as a reminder of skills that may need to be taught or retaught. In addition, the profile afforded by the individual record for each child is usually so informative that it may easily be used during teacher-parent conferences as well as teacher-pupil conferences.

As soon as the teacher has acquired competence and confidence with a small group using individualized reading, it is possible to include another group. This process may be extended until all pupils are involved in the new arrangement.

Chapter 8

Utilizing a Learning-
Center Setting

Learning centers are found in many elementary and secondary schools. They vary in terms of space, materials, personnel, and scheduled use; however, the intent to foster individualization of instruction is common to all.

It is the purpose of this chapter to describe learning centers and to suggest how they may be utilized in the individualized reading approach. This is not to be viewed as an instructional substitute; rather, it should be considered an adjunct to the classroom teacher's reading program.

Types of Learning-Center Settings

The learning center is essentially an environment, an organization of people and materials in a suitable setting, designed to activate pupils' interests and to meet their identified needs. There are several types of settings that have proved to be suitable and effective:

1. A small classroom, staffed by a clerk or teacher's aide, containing ten to twelve individual carrels and appropriate equipment and materials (either in the carrels or on shelves) for pupils assigned to the center for specific purposes.
2. A larger classroom, carpeted and airconditioned, staffed by a teacher and one or more aides, containing at least five tables and thirty chairs, closets or cabinets and shelves for storage, and a variety of books, audio-visual equipment and materials, and skills-development workbooks and games.
3. A double classroom (usually created by removing the partition between two rooms), carpeted and airconditioned, containing six to twelve individual carrels, several tables with chairs around them, a few lounge chairs or carpeted benches to form a quiet corner, closets or cabinets and shelves for storage, and a variety of materials and equipment—usually

staffed by a teacher and one or more aides but sometimes staffed by a team of teachers for an interdisciplinary approach to learning.

4. A section of the school library, containing essentially the items listed in item 2 or item 3 above.

5. A wing or section of the school, approximately the size of four classrooms, containing several partitioned conference or study rooms in addition to the items listed in item 3 above.

6. An entire building used specifically for the purpose of individualization, staffed by teachers and aides who plan together how to involve children individually or in small groups in activities which will sustain their interests and meet their needs.

The creative educator who understands individualization of instruction as interests- and needs-meeting may grasp the significance of item 6 above. With changes in philosophy and retraining of existing school staffs, it is possible to turn existing school plants into learning centers that enable children to become independent learners and to achieve in terms of their capabilities.

Observed Uses of Learning Centers
For Reading Growth

The uses of learning centers vary considerably from school to school. Activities scheduled for the learning center depend on the philosophy of the school staff. There is evidence that most faculties have selected reading-skills development as an important component of their centers.

Many schools provide opportunities for children to go to learning centers at suitable times, usually assigned, for free reading and use of audio-visual materials. Others have developed schedules so that classroom teachers may take an entire class to the learning center for several days or weeks.

In some instances, the classroom teacher makes all decisions concerning the activities from which pupils may choose what they wish to do. In other cases, the classroom teacher teams with a specialist (reading, language arts, media, or curriculum) to plan activities appropriate for particular groups of children. At times, after children have become acquainted with the center, they may plan and carry out activities of their own choice.

Many classroom teachers who carry on an individualized reading program spend several hours in the learning center before they send pupils there. They study the materials, locate audio-visual aids that relate to their on-going programs, and learn the procedures involved. They receive assistance from the teacher responsible for the center, especially in the identification of skills-development materials and the location of stories and books available for independent reading. This is a valuable use of the learning center, for the classroom teacher updates his knowledge of materials and satisfies himself that the center is a suitable environment for fostering and extending individualized reading.

In instances where reading teachers have begun to view their facilities as a multisensory learning center, they have made their room available to more children. At the same time that some children report for teacher-directed reading instruction, other children may report to carry out self-directed activities. A simple reporting or scheduling system, discussed later in this chapter, seems to provide adequate controls of the movement of children.

Two distinct and separate uses of learning-center settings as adjuncts to individualized reading programs appear to have emerged in actual practice:

1. Children make their own decisions about the use of the learning center, including times of going, purposes to be achieved, and materials to be used. These children learn the procedures, receive instruction in location and use of materials and equipment, and maintain good communication with the center staff as well as their own teachers. They become independent to the degree possible in a setting utilized by many children and for many purposes.

2. Teachers accompany or send groups of children to the learning center at times suitable to both the center and the ongoing classroom schedule. Usually, after careful diagnosis of specific pupils' needs, the teacher suggests the general skill or topic to be pursued on a specific day. A variety of materials is listed, permitting individual pupils to select one that interests them. Occasionally, a teacher lists a specific material, knowing that it will meet a pupil's needs and hold his interest. Pupils advise their teacher when they have completed an activity.

As the learning-center setting becomes feasible in more schools, individualized reading teachers may come to view the center as a real extension of their classrooms. Expensive equipment and materials may be more readily available to more children, and teachers may

Schedule for Use of the Learning Center

School Year _____ Weekly Schedule for _____
                                                              (month)

| Daily Schedule | | Assignment of Five Groups of Six Pupils Per Hour | | | | |
Day	Time	Teacher	Teacher	Teacher	Teacher	Teacher
Monday	8-9	Mr. Smith	OPEN			
	9-10	OPEN				
	10-11	Miss Green				
	11-12	Mrs. Coats				OPEN
	12-1	Miss Jones			OPEN	
	1-2	Mrs. Frye		OPEN		
	2-3	Mr. Nix				
Tuesday	8-9	Mr. Smith				
	9-10	Mrs. Frye				OPEN
	10-11	Miss Green			OPEN	
	11-12	Mrs. Coats				
	12-1	Miss Jones		OPEN		
	1-2	OPEN				
	2-3	Mr. Nix	OPEN			
Wednesday	8-9	OPEN				
	9-10	Mr. Smith			OPEN	
	10-11	Miss Green		OPEN		
	11-12	Mrs. Coats				
	12-1	Miss Jones	OPEN			
	1-2	Mrs. Frye				
	2-3	Mr. Nix				OPEN
Thursday	8-9	Mr. Smith			OPEN	
	9-10	Miss Jones		OPEN		
	10-11	Miss Green	OPEN			
	11-12	OPEN				
	12-1	Mrs. Coats				
	1-2	Mrs. Frye				OPEN
	2-3	Mr. Nix				
Friday	8-9	Mr. Smith		OPEN		
	9-10	Mr. Nix	OPEN			
	10-11	Miss Green				OPEN
	11-12	Mrs. Coats				
	12-1	Miss Jones				
	1-2	Mrs. Frye			OPEN	
	2-3	OPEN				

Teachers wishing to assign six pupils during any time period marked OPEN should request the time at least one day prior to expected assignment. The request may be handled by sending a pupil with a note stating date and time; the center will respond immediately with either acceptance of the suggested time or indication of another available time if the desired time has been assigned.

Figure 9.

reduce greatly the number of problems encountered in locating materials and keeping records. The element of management, the next consideration of this chapter, will become as routine as other aspects of the individualized reading approach. This does not imply that there should be fewer reading materials in the classroom; however, it may be possible to reduce to some degree the number of audio-visual materials and skills-development workbooks and games.

Essential Records for Assignment of Pupils to A Learning Center

Communication between the classroom teacher and the staff of the learning center may be a critical factor to maximum development of individualized reading. In connection with pupils' reading growth, good communication is essential, for the progress of children depends on the teacher's knowing what they are doing and how well they are performing.

At the beginning of the year, faculties work out the details for scheduling pupils to centers. The individualized reading teacher may request specific time periods if all teachers are to be scheduled in that fashion.

Figure 9 shows a possible schedule for teacher- and/or pupil-assignment to a learning center. In this example, designation of teachers has been shown for only one section; it will be noted that six teachers have been scheduled to send six pupils each day for five days, with only one variation in time for some teachers. This variation indicates that on specific days certain teachers have prior commitments. The schedule also shows that certain sections are left unassigned so that teachers may have an opportunity to send special groups as there is need.

In the event that teachers are not regularly scheduled for specific times, the learning-center staff may maintain a similar assignment schedule on which to keep a record of teachers' requests. It is necessary to maintain some type of schedule if facilities are limited, and teachers need to know how the center staff expects to control the numbers of children working in the center.

Keeping a record of children's visits to the center may be important in evaluating the services of the center to the school. Therefore, some type of book should be placed where children may "sign in" when they arrive at the center. An entry similar to that given in Figure 10 may be sufficient:

Visitors to the Learning Center

Date	Time	Name	Reason for Coming
9/11	8:15	Billy Smith	To find a filmstrip about frogs
9/11	8:20	Mary Green	To practice reading blends
9/11	8:21	John Cox	To read my own book

Figure 10.

It may be necessary to include the name of the pupil's teacher in some instances. Also, a "sign out" time may be added for schools that require more rigid control of pupils' movements.

It should be clear that, if groups of children are regularly assigned, this type of record would not be needed; nor would it be practical. If, however, individual children go to the center without being scheduled, a record similar to this may be suitable to record their visits. An important training factor will be observed if children learn the reasons for signing the record and if they are praised for following this instruction. Details of this kind must be worked out carefully so that all school personnel know the procedures to be followed.

For the purposes of the individualized reading program, the most essential record is the pupil's record of what he accomplished at the center. A form similar to that shown in Figure 11, entitled "My Report of Activities at the Learning Center," may be used. This may be a card or a sheet or paper containing the information.

Prior to leaving his classroom, the pupil should fill in his name, the date, and the time he expects to go. He should also complete part A to indicate his intent, partly to create in himself a mind set for a specific activity and partly to provide information for the teacher and the center staff. If the form were to serve as a "pass" to the center, the information would inform other school personnel of the pupil's intent.

Upon completion of his activities in the center, the pupil should complete at least part B of the report. If there is need for additional information that the child cannot write himself, a member of the center staff could supply needed details on the back of the card. Part C may be completed at the center or at a later time, perhaps during a teacher-pupil conference. Completed reports should be filed with other pupil's reports of reading.

At times, the teacher may encourage children to evaluate their own performance in activities carried out at the center and to record

My Report of Activities at the Learning Center

Pupil _____ From _____ room

Date _____ Time _____ (teacher or number)

A. I plan to do this at the center: _____

_____

_____

B. At the center, I did this: _____

_____

_____

_____

C. I want to go to the center again to _____

_____

_____

Figure 11.

a symbol on the card to indicate their progress. A code such as the following may be sufficient:

√√ for "very good"   √ for "satisfactory"

?   for "don't know"   x for "too hard" or "not interesting"

The encouragement of children to evaluate their own performance requires opportunities for honest and honorable statements, comments that a child may make without feeling that he is downgrading himself. For that reason, it is logical to use a code that enables him to report his achievement in terms that are acceptable to him. When a child did not perform well, the chances are that the activity was indeed "too hard" or "not interesting."

The teacher may incorporate these reports with other pupil reports on the individual record of "Quantitative Summary of Individual Reading" (see Figure 3). There will then be a full summary of the activities in which the individual pupil has engaged.

The purpose of the records described in this chapter must be kept in mind. They are intended to provide needed information for learning-center staff and classroom teachers engaged in an extension of the individualized reading approach. Different types of records may be needed for reporting teacher-directed work in a learning center.

Anticipated Results of Extending
The Reading Program to Include
Learning-Center Activities

It is difficult to know precisely all benefits which may result from extending any reading program. For the individualized reading approach, it is believed that at least the following will be evident:

1. Teachers will have access to additional materials and equipment for inclusion in their reading programs.
2. Pupils will increase their self-selection skills.
3. Pupils will have opportunities to use materials and equipment not normally available to them.
4. Pupils will have opportunities for interaction with children of various ages, thereby increasing their communication skills.
5. Pupils will discover that many children have needs and interests similar to theirs.
6. Pupils will develop skills in self-direction in a different environment.
7. Pupils will have improved self-concepts because they carry out new responsibilities.

Chapter 9

Stepping Toward
Individualizing

Because every class is unique, the classroom teacher is usually the person best qualified to determine the manner in which his pupils should be initiated and directed into an individualized reading program. What one teacher has found workable and convenient in his situation may not be appropriate in another.

It is helpful, in many instances, for teachers contemplating the use of individualized reading practices to have a guide or reference to serve them in making adaptations to a different type of reading design. For this reason, the following outline is offered as an example that may be useful.

Step 1: Selection of Books

Boys and girls should have a special time to locate good books when they have the counsel of teachers and librarians. At first, before a regular time has been established, the period usually devoted to small ability-grouped reading may be used for book selections and free reading.

Illustration

"We are going to use the next 45 minutes to find some good books to read. As soon as you have found something interesting from the selection on our shelves or from the school library, please use your time to read. I hope you will ask me to help you find a good book if you have any trouble finding one about a topic you like."

Step 2: The Teacher's Function

Pupils need to know what the teacher plans to do while they are reading. This permits them to prepare for reading with the teacher as well as to enjoy their own self-selected reading material alone.

Illustration

"During the reading period, I would like some of you to read with me. It should be interesting to know what kinds of books you like, how well you read them, and some things you have learned from your books."

Step 3: Selection of Pupils to Read Individually

For ease of operation, it is important to explain exactly how pupils will be selected to read individually with the teacher.

Illustration

"A few minutes after you have begun to read, I would like to have some of you join me for a while and tell me something about the book you are reading. Jane, suppose you sit with me at our library table. It's very comfortable back there and far enough from the others that our talking should not disturb them. When Jane has read with me, I will have her walk quietly to someone who seems to be ready and ask him to join me at the library table with his book. If you are not ready, say so, and we will find someone else and call on you tomorrow or some other time."

Step 4: Reasons for a Teacher-Pupil Conference

The teacher must inform his pupils why he wishes to have them read to him and with him individually. The teacher should also let his pupils know something about the nature of the individual conference with the teacher.

Illustration

"Sometimes we choose books for reading that are too easy and at other times we may choose books to read that are too difficult. When you read with me, I not only enjoy being with you and learning about your book, but I get a chance to know how well you read the book that you have selected. When we meet, I expect to make notes that will call my attention to things we need to do so that you may become a better reader. This is what I will usually ask you to do for me:

1. Read some part of the book orally that you select and read a small portion that I select.

2. Read a portion of your book silently so that I may ask you questions about what you read.
3. Re-read words that caused difficulty or passages that were not very well explained.
4. Talk with me about the part you have read and make judgments about sections that you haven't read."

Step 5: The Pupil's Record-Keeping Responsibility

It should be explained that each pupil has a certain record-keeping responsibility which includes entering on a proper form the books he has read and other information desired by the teacher.

Illustration

"For your use there are some forms entitled 'Student's Record of Personal Reading.' Whenever you complete a book, a story in a book of stories, or other articles you wish to record, please fill in one of the forms and put it in the box that has a copy of that form attached to the cover."

Step 6: Plans For Skill Development

In order to assure continuous development of skills in word attack and reading, a definite time should be devoted to this task. It may be a daily period following free reading, or it might be a period arranged for fewer days per school week. A checklist of basic word-attack and comprehension skills similar to the one listed in this booklet may be helpful to the teacher who wants to be sure that the essentials are considered in his class.

Illustration

"On Mondays, Wednesdays, and Fridays we should have a reading skills lesson to be sure everyone is growing in the use of many aids in the improvement of reading. Sometimes I may wish to work on a skill the whole class needs. Sometimes I may work with individuals or small groups. The notes I take during our conferences help me decide the things we need to learn.

"Let's begin now. Do you see the small words on the chart? Perhaps a different person might pronounce each one for us. (Have children pronounce hid, kit, sit, fat, and other monosyllables representing closed syllables and all vowels having the short sound.) Very well done. These are easy words, and I didn't think you would mispronounce any of them. Now let's place on the end of each of these an 'e' and then pronounce them. Good. What have you noticed about the change in sound? (Response) The 'e' tells us to use a long vowel sound."

Follow by providing other examples, having students use examples of their own, and re-evaluating. Note those who still need help on the specific skill under consideration.

Step 7: Plans for Reading in Small Groups

Many children like to belong to a group for reading. Teachers of individualized reading should plan some time for small-group reading. Groups may be formed for one of three general types of reading. It is worthwhile occasionally to have a small group meet to discuss books they are reading and possibly read selected portions to the group under the supervision of the teacher or a group leader. Small groups may be formed to read from the same book or about the same general theme from different books.

Illustration

"I remember that some of you are especially interested in dinosaurs and prehistoric man. There are six books on these topics available in the room. They came from some of your homes, the library, and my personal collection. I would like to have some of you who are interested to meet with me for about 20 minutes to examine these books, discuss them, and read small parts to give us all some ideas about them. Raise your hand if you would like to join me."

Step 8: Development of Reading and Work Habits

Some boys and girls need closer supervision when working alone than do others. Many can function better in a team or with a partner. Guidelines for using the reading period should be explained to the class.

Illustration

"When you are reading alone or working with others, remember your friends and classmates. Be considerate and avoid disturbing others who are reading and working in the room. We should learn to be good judges of things to do during our reading and work periods. Try to read silently unless you need to quietly sound a new word to help get its meaning. You can read more and faster silently than orally. If you are with a friend, find a place to work where your conversation and activities are not distracting to others. I will try to be ready to help you if you seem to need me."

Step 9: Integration of Prior Steps

After children have had guidance in the various phases of the individualized reading approach, the teacher may wish to explain the procedures to be followed in the future. In this way, prior steps are reviewed, and the totality of the new program can be made clear. It should be anticipated that various aspects of the approach will need to be reviewed periodically with individuals or small groups.

Illustration

"For several days now, we have been developing skills and procedures for reading and working independently. We know how to locate interesting materials to read, and we have learned how to take care of these materials. You have discovered that I work with some of you individually sometimes and with small groups at other times. I believe you realize that I am placing responsibility on each of you to select your materials and to ask for help when you need it.

"In our conferences, we have talked about stories, read parts of them, and planned things to do. You have learned to fill out the forms to report your reading. This provides a record for you and for me. Then, you have discovered that I plan for special groups, some for skill development and some for sharing of reading.

"I can see that you are learning good reading and work habits so that we may continue with this individualized plan. We shall continue to work in this way during the year. As we discover ways to share and to learn together, we shall include other activities."

Step 10: Extension Beyond the Regular Classroom

If there is a reading or learning center in the school, the teacher may wish to permit children to go to the center to utilize special materials not available in the classroom. It is important to have clear understandings that the choice to go to the center is the child's choice. It is equally important that the child know what to expect in the center, including the materials available and the processes to be followed.

Illustration

"Today, several of you may go to the reading (or learning) center. There is a teacher's aide there who can help you locate tapes, records, filmstrips, or books on topics you are interested in. You may use the materials there, and you will be shown how to operate any equipment that you need. Of course, you must be careful to follow instructions, but I am sure you can.

"I visited the center last week, and I know there are many books, workbooks, tapes, and other materials that we do not have in our room or in the library. If you know what you would like to read about or to learn to do, you will have no trouble getting something interesting. But it is important for you to know what you would like to do before you go to the center.

"You need not feel that you must plan to go to the center today or any other time. We are simply making these extra materials available to you if you want to go.

"The only thing you will need to record for me will be a card, one much like the one you now use to report on your reading in the room. I have the cards in this box by the door (demonstrating). You will take a card and fill out part of it before you leave the room. I want you to plan ahead of time what you want to do in the learning center; you can write a brief statement of that on the card. After you finish your activities in the center, you will finish the card, just as you do when you finish reading in the room.

"At the center, you will sign your name in a special book for visitors and write after your name what you are interested in doing. You may ask for help from the teachers or aides at the center. Be sure you wait until someone is free to help you.

"Now, how many of you would like to go today? If there are more than six, some may go another time, probably tomorrow. Then, we shall make it possible for others to go next week. If we like this arrangement, we can have the privilege often."

Bibliography

Archer, H.P. "Individualizing Reading: Hard, but Worth It," *Grade Teacher*, 85 (September, 1967), 118-19.

Aronow, Miriam S. "A Study of the Effects of Individualized Reading on Children's Reading Test Scores," *The Reading Teacher*, 15 (November, 1961), 86-92.

Askov, E.N. "Instrument for Assessing Teachers' Attitudes Toward Individualizing Reading Instruction," *Journal of Experimental Education*, 39 (Spring, 1971), 5-10.

Barbe, Walter B. *Educator's Guide to Personalized Reading Instruction*. Englewood Cliffs, New Jersey, Prentice-Hall, Inc., 1961.

Berretta, S. "Self-Concept Development in the Reading Program," *The Reading Teacher*, 24 (December, 1970), 232-38.

Blakely, W. Paul, and McKay, Beverly. "Individualized Reading as Part of an Eclectic Reading Program," *Elementary English*, 43 (March, 1966), 214-19.

Brogan, Peggy, and Fox, Lorene K. *Helping Children Read*. New York, Holt, Rinehart & Winston, Inc., 1961.

Cadenhead, Kenneth. "A Plan for Individualizing Reading Instruction," *Elementary English*, 39 (March, 1962), 260-62.

Crossley, Ruth, and Kniley, Mildred. "An Individual Reading Program," *Elementary English*, 36 (January, 1959), 16-20.

Daniels, P.R. "Learning Centers and Stations: A Different Concept," *AV Instructor*, 15 (November, 1970), 29.

Darrow, Helen F., and Howes, Virgil M. *Approaches to Individualized Reading*. New York, Appleton-Century-Crofts, 1960.

Davis, F.W., and Lucas, J.S. "Experiment in Individualized Reading," *The Reading Teacher*, 24 (May, 1971), 737-43.

Dolch, E.W. "Individualized Reading vs. Group Reading II," *Elementary English*, 39 (January, 1962), 14-21, 32.

Duker, Sam. *Individualized Reading: An Annotated Bibliography*. Metuchen, New Jersey, Scarecrow Press, 1968.

Duker, Sam. "Masters' Studies of Individualized Reading," *Elementary English*, 47 (May, 1970), 655-60.

Evans, N. Dean. "Individualized Reading—Myths and Facts," *Elementary English*, 39 (October, 1962), 580-83.

Fisch, Muriel. "Record Keeping for Individualized Reading," *Grade Teacher*, 76 (November, 1958), 90-91, 93.

Folcarelli, J. "Don't Be Afraid of Individualized Reading," *Grade Teacher*, 84 (November, 1966), 110.

Fried, G.E. "Learning Center Approach to Language Improvement," *Reading Improvement*, 7 (Fall, 1970), 51-53.

Gans, Roma. *Common Sense in Teaching Reading*. Indianapolis, Indiana, Bobbs-Merrill Co., Inc., 1963.

Green, C. "Individual Approach to Reading," *The Texas Outlook*, 52 (October, 1968), 627-33.

Groff, Patrick J. "A Check on Individualized Reading," *Education*, 84 (March, 1964), 397-401.

Groff, Patrick J. "Comparisons of Individualized and Ability-Grouping Approaches to Reading Achievement," *Elementary English*, 40 (March, 1963), 258-64, 276.

Groff, Patrick J. "Materials for Individualized Reading," *Elementary English*, 38 (January, 1961), 1-7.

Grotberg, E.H. "Individualized Reading: A Symbol for Change," *Education*, 87 (September, 1966), 7-11.

Gurney, David. "The Effect of an Individual Reading Program on Reading Level and Attitude Toward Reading," *The Reading Teacher*, 19 (January, 1966), 277-80.

Harris, Albert (Ed.). *Readings on Reading Instruction*. New York, David McKay Company, Inc., 1963.

Heilman, Arthur W. *Principles and Practices of Teaching Reading*, 2nd Ed. Columbus, Ohio, Charles E. Merrill Books, Inc., 1967.

Hostetter, Beverly. "What Does Individualized Reading Mean to You?" *Elementary English*, 39 (March, 1962), 263-65.

Howes, Virgil M. *Individualizing Instruction in Reading and Social Studies* (Selected Readings on Programs and Practices). New York, The Macmillan Company, 1970.

Howes, Virgil M., and Darrow, Helen (Eds.). *Reading and the Elementary School Child*. New York, The Macmillan Company, 1968.

Hunt, Lyman C. "Effect of Self-Selection, Interest, and Motivation Upon Independent, Instructional, and Frustration Levels," *The Reading Teacher*, 24 (November, 1970), 146-51.

Hunt, Lyman C. (Ed.). *The Individualized Program: A Guide for*

Classroom Teaching. Newark, Delaware, International Reading Association, 1966.

Hunt, Lyman C. "Six Steps to the Individualized Reading Program," *Elementary English,* 48 (January, 1971), 27-32.

Karlin, Robert. "Some Reactions to Individualized Reading," *The Reading Teacher,* 11 (December, 1957), 95-98.

Keener, B.M. "Individualized Reading and the Disadvantaged," *The Reading Teacher,* 20 (February, 1967), 410-12.

Lazar, May. "Individualized Reading, A Dynamic Approach," *The Reading Teacher,* 11 (December, 1957), 75-83.

Lofthourse, Yvonne. "Individualized Reading: Significant Research," *The Reading Teacher,* 16 (September, 1962), 36-38.

MacDonald, J.B. "Individual Vs. Group Instruction in First Grade Reading," *The Reading Teacher,* 19 (May, 1966), 643-46.

Sister Mary Marita. "Beginning Reading Achievement in Three Classroom Organizational Patterns," *The Reading Teacher,* 20 (October, 1966), 12-17.

McVey, Marcia. "Individualized Vs. Independent Reading," *Education,* 82 (September, 1961), 17-18.

Meil, Alice (Ed.). "Individualizing Reading Practices," No. 14, *Practical Suggestions for Teaching.* New York, Bureau of Publications, Teachers College, Columbia University, 1959.

Mellen, M.E. "Individualizing: To Stimulate the Slow Reader," *Grade Teacher,* 85 (March, 1968), 109-10.

Miller, W.H. "Organizing a First Grade Classroom for Individual Reading Instruction," *The Reading Teacher,* 24 (May, 1971), 748-52.

Odom, S. "Individualizing a Reading Program," *The Reading Teacher,* 24 (February, 1971), 403-10.

Posner, A.N. "Individualized Reading," *Education,* 82 (November, 1961), 183-86.

Ramsey, Wallace (Ed.). *Organizing for Individual Differences.* Newark, Delaware, International Reading Association, 1967.

Sandberg, Herbert H. (Ed). *Educational Comment on Individual Reading.* Toledo, Ohio, The University of Toledo, College of Education, 1966.

Sartain, Harry W. "A Bibliography on Individualized Reading," *The Reading Teacher,* 12 (April, 1960), 262-65, 270.

Sartain, Harry W. "Research on Individualized Reading," *Education,* 81 (May, 1961), 515-21.

Sartain, Harry W. "The Roseville Experiment with Individualized Reading," *The Reading Teacher,* 13 (April, 1960), 277-81.

Savage, J.F. "Teaching Reading with the Aid of Technology," *A V Instructor*, 15 (November, 1970), 24-25.

Schatz, Esther; Utterback, Roberta; Wilsbert, Mary; and Frazier, Alexander. *Exploring Independent Reading in the Primary Grades*. Bulletin from College of Education, Ohio State University, Columbus, Ohio, 1960.

Schubert, Delwyn G., and Torgerson, Theodore. *Improving Reading Through Individualized Correction*, 2nd Ed. Dubuque, Iowa, W.C. Brown Co., 1968.

Sharpe, Maida Wood. "Individualized Reading: Follow-up Activities," *Elementary English*, 36 (January, 1959), 21-23.

Smith, Nila Banton. *Reading for Today's Children*. Englewood Cliffs, New Jersey, Prentice-Hall, Inc., 1963.

Spache, George D. *Good Reading for Poor Readers*. Champaign, Illinois, Garrard Publishing Co., 1966.

Spencer, D.V. "Individualized First Grade Reading Vs. a Basal Reader Program in Rural Communities," *The Reading Teacher*, 19 (May, 1966), 595-600.

Staiger, Ralph C. "Some Aspects of Individualized Reading," *Education*, 80 (May, 1960), 527-29.

Stauffer, Russell G. *Teaching Reading as a Thinking Process*. New York, Harper & Row, Publishers, 1969.

Stuart, Allaire. "Individualized Reading," *Elementary English*, 39 (March, 1962), 255-59.

Swafford, Alton L. "Evaluation of an Individualized Reading Program," *The Reading Teacher*, 13 (April, 1960), 266-70.

Thomas, George I., and Crescimbini, Joseph. *Individualizing Instruction in the Elementary School*. New York, Random House, 1967.

Trusty, K. "Principles of Learning and Individualized Reading," *The Reading Teacher*, 24 (May, 1971), 730-39.

Veatch, Jeannette. *Individualizing Your Reading Program: Self-Selection in Action*. New York, Putnam, 1959.

Veatch, Jeannette. *Reading in the Elementary School*. New York, Ronald Press, 1966.

Vite, Irene W. "Individualized Reading—The Scoreboard on Control Studies," *Education*, 81 (January, 1961), 285-90.

Wilberg, L., and Trost, M. "Comparison Between the Content of First Grade Primers and the Free Choice Library Selections Made by First Grade Students," *Elementary English*, 47 (October, 1970), 792-98.

Wilson, Richard C. "Using Individualized Reading as a Diagnostic Technique," in Dorothy L. DeBoer (Ed.), *Reading Diagnosis and*

Evaluation. Newark, Delaware, International Reading Association, 1970.

Wilson, Richard C., and Harrison, Robert. "Skill Growth With Individualized Reading," *Elementary English*, 40 (April, 1963), 433-35.

Witty, Paul A. "Individualized Reading: A Postscript," *Elementary English*, 41 (March, 1964), 211-17.

Wolf, M. "Individualized Reading: How I Broke the Mold: Third Grade Reading Program," *Grade Teacher*, 87 (September, 1969), 158.